Dear Susan & Ray,

Just a little glimpse of our slice of heaven — New Hampshire!

♡ The Dolfis

NEW HAMPSHIRE

A Photographic Journey

Photographs by

Robert J. Kozlow

HUNTINGTON GRAPHICS
Burlington, Vermont

Published by Huntington Graphics
PO Box 373, Burlington, VT 05402
www.huntingtongraphics.com

Copyright © 2010 Huntington Graphics
Copyright © 2010 photographs Robert J. Kozlow

Cover photo: Squam Lake from Mount Morgan, Holderness, New Hampshire

Printed in Canada

ISBN 978-1-886064-36-2

Contents

.

Acknowledgments

Many people were instrumental in the creation of this book. Jared Gange, my publisher, worked for many hours to compile my best images into an artistic format. Sarah Semler pored through many slide sheets and digital files, and Emery Hard spent time editing the text.

The employees of the New Hampshire State Park system as well as the many people who operate our tourist attractions deserve special recognition. In particular, Mike Pelchat, Bill and Jayne O'Connor, Amy Bassett, Howie Weymess, and Dexter Rust have all been very supportive, and often helped me reach my photo locations in a pinch. I would also like to thank the Mount Washington Observatory and Dr. Peter Crane for helping me obtain the Mount Washington images.

Special thanks go to all my friends and hiking partners who accompanied me on this photographic journey and who appear throughout the book, most notably Christopher O'Leary, Daniel Hultgren, Andrew and Patrick Keefer, Alex Kent, Michael Benton, Mark Hollenbach, and my very dear friend Shaun Moe.

I am grateful to John Harrigan for his foreword. People all over the state love John's newspaper columns, as he is an avid spokesman for all that we find unique and wonderful about New Hampshire.

I would also like to thank Steve Smith and Mike Dickerman for their unwavering support over the years. Special recognition goes to my professional colleagues, who supported me during both of my photography projects. In particular, I would like to thank the Dental Resource Center at LRGHealthcare and my Meredith office staff. Thank you, Kelly Beddia for being a good listener and faithful friend.

Finally, I dedicate this book to my parents, Donna Kozlow and the late Joseph Kozlow, whose love, patience, and encouragement made this project possible. It has truly been a labor of love on this wonderful journey through God's country.

— Robert J. Kozlow
Gilford, New Hampshire

Foreword

People who've been fortunate enough to have roamed New Hampshire from Coös to the Sea will recognize many a place, theme and pursuit in Bob Kozlow's second fine book on the myriad sights and experiences to be found along the state's highways and byways—and far off the beaten path as well. Those who haven't poked around this wonderful piece of geography—high country, valleys, woods, field, forest, streams, lakes and ponds—will look through this book and just plain want to pack up, get out, and go.

Coming on the heels of his first grand photographic compilation, *The White Mountains, A Photographic Journey,* Bob's latest addition to the publishing scene, *New Hampshire—A Photographic Journey* offers a past that is still very much with us and a present and future offering enjoyment for anyone with a map, an appreciation for great diversity and beauty, and the time to get out and look.

From a technical standpoint, the book's photographic reproduction is stunning. The definition and colors are so crisp and clear that they practically jump off the pages. Rarely does a photography book come along with such excellence of quality.

Equally stunning, perhaps even more so, is the thought, time, perseverance and hard work that Bob put into obtaining so many truly one-of-a-kind images. Even the most casual, decidedly amateur photographer has only to look at the cloud formations, blue sky, silky waterfalls and brilliant foliage so abundant in Bob's photographs to appreciate the incredible foresight, knowledge of terrain, experience with the seasons, and commitment to untold weather-related return trips so evident in the spectacular results.

How did he manage to do that—catch it just right? The answer, of course, is thorough knowledge of his subjects, vast experience on back roads, waterways and high-country trails, and the sharp eye and attention to detail requisite for the making of any truly good picture.

Here we have working boats off New Hampshire's all-too-meager coast, a living link to the past. There we have the Thomas Laighton, steaming ahead with a boatload of tourists. Three rugged tugs are tied up in Portsmouth, with bricks and belfry for a background. And on up the state we go. A solitary hiker looks out at the panorama of Lake Winnipesaukee and beyond. Skiers trudge up toward Tuckerman's awesome headwall. Kayakers make their fleeting marks on the Saco. A covered bridge, church and graveyard present a timeless scene in Stark. Clouds and countryside sweep away around the Keazer Farm in Colebrook. Within sight of Lower Canada, loons swim and tall trees bend to the wind.

Here, then, is a delightful invitation to see, explore, appreciate, experience and enjoy, whether by car, bike, canoe or on foot. If you know and love New Hampshire, and want others to share the joy and beauty of it all, this book is for you.

— John Harrigan
Colebrook, New Hampshire

The Seacoast

With only 18 miles of oceanfront, New Hampshire's seacoast has a remarkable number of historical sites, fine inns and restaurants, and cultural events. The coastal communities differ in industry and ambience, ranging from Portsmouth, settled in 1630 as the colonial capital, to Hampton Beach, which became one of New England's most popular seaside resorts after the development of the electric trolley in the nineteenth century. Between these two extremes, many small towns dot the seacoast with their white churches and town commons.

Wallis Sands State Park in Rye is one of several sandy beaches along Route 1A that attract vacationers to the seacoast.

Appledore Island, one of the nine Isles of Shoals, is home to the University of New Hampshire marine biology program.

The Portsmouth Harbor Lighthouse, built in 1877, stands on the site of the American Colonies' first light station north of Boston.

Wentworth by the Sea, one of New Hampshire's historic grand hotels, once hosted socialites, film stars, presidents, and even the peace talks that ended the Russo-Japanese War. Recently renovated by the Marriott Hotel chain, this 161-room resort hotel overlooks the Atlantic Ocean from a high bluff.

As the state capital during the American Revolution, a former textile mill town, and the current home of Phillips Exeter Academy, Exeter boasts a great diversity of architecture.

Star Island's modern ferry, the Thomas Laighton, is a replica of the steamships that hauled passengers and freight to this popular summer colony at the turn of the twentieth century.

Throughout its patchwork history, Star Island has attracted pirates, writers, fishermen, artists, and naturalists to the Isles of Shoals.

Founded in 1866 as a school for agriculture and the mechanical arts, the University of New Hampshire in Durham now offers a broad-based curriculum.

The White Island Lighthouse, located beside the childhood home of author Celia Thaxter, once guided writers like Nathaniel Hawthorne and artists such as the American Impressionist Childe Hassam to its rocky shore.

Hampton Beach lies quiet at night, though more than 200,000 people can cover the oceanfront during peak summer weekends.

Portsmouth's famous tugs are hardworking vessels that smooth the way for everything from oil tankers and atomic subs to tall ships navigating the Piscataqua River's fast and challenging tides.

Lakes Region

At 24 miles long and up to 15 miles wide, Winnipesaukee is New Hampshire's largest lake. Its 274 habitable islands and 72 square miles of deep, spring-fed water provide a unique playground for athletes and summer vacationers alike. In addition to the region's many destinations for swimming, sailing, and paddling, places like Lake Sunapee and Meredith offer summer theater productions and numerous hiking trails. From the summits of mountains like Kearsarge and Cardigan, the region sparkles like a constellation below.

With its 283 miles of shoreline, Lake Winnipesaukee draws visitors to the Lakes Region in all seasons. Scenic cruises, swimming, and boating fill the summer months, while skiers, ice fishermen, and snowmobilers arrive when the autumn foliage gives way to winter.

Billed as America's oldest summer resort, Wolfeboro remains a popular vacation spot with its quaint harbor and old-fashioned charm.

Nestled in the foothills of the White Mountains, Newfound Lake's spring-fed water makes it one of the clearest and cleanest in the United States.

The Bear Island Post Office awaits its daily delivery from the M/V Sophie C., whose mail route snakes about several Lake Winnipesaukee islands.

An eight-foot bronze statue of Chief Chocorua stands on Indian Island in Meredith Bay, honoring the Native American cultures that shaped the history of the Lakes Region.

Canaan Street Lake offers a small town beach where residents and tourists alike gather to fish, swim, and boat during the warm summer months.

The Squam Lakes Association, nestled at the head of this little bay, provides recreational and educational opportunities at its lakeside head-quarters, and also maintains many of the hiking trails in the region.

Settled in 1779, Ancestral Acres uses a wood-fired evaporator to produce maple syrup, cream, and sugar at its scenic mountaintop farm in New Hampton.

Benton's Sugar Shack in Thornton operates a family-owned restaurant offering weekend breakfasts as well as information about the process of maple sugaring.

Floating down the Squam River, the principal boating access for Squam Lake, travelers enjoy views of Red Hill in the distance.

Boasting a network of ski trails originally designed by Franklin D. Roosevelt's WPA, Gunstock Mountain has drawn visitors to Gilford since 1937 with its family-friendly terrain and stunning views.

As winter settles on Meredith Village, the bay becomes a destination for ice fishing and snowmobiling.

Picnic Rock Farms in Meredith is famous for its fresh vegetables, fruit, baked goods, and maple syrup. The farm has been in the same family since 1801.

A classic wooden boat casts a rainbow in its wake on Squam Lake in Holderness.

Dating back to 1916, Laconia Race Week is the oldest motorcycle rally in the nation. In recent years, Weirs Beach has hosted 375,000 motorcyclists over the nine-day event, making the celebration New Hampshire's largest annual event.

Just off the northern shore of Newfound Lake, Loon Island invites early-morning boaters to contemplate its natural beauty.

The M/S Mount Washington offers daily cruises on Lake Winnipesaukee. This famous vessel has plied the lake since 1940.

Built on Ossipee Mountain in 1913, the 5,500-acre Castle in the Clouds estate now attracts visitors with its waterfalls, outstanding gardens, and 30 miles of trails.

From the summit of Mount Sunapee, the ten-mile-long and three-mile-wide expanse of Lake Sunapee shimmers below, sheathed almost entirely in green.

Sitting on the 3,121-foot summit of Mount Cardigan, hikers enjoy panoramic views that encompass the White Mountains to the north, Camels Hump in Vermont, and Maine's Pleasant Mountain.

With a population of 20,000, Laconia is the largest community in the Lakes Region. The Belknap Mill, built in 1823, is the oldest unaltered textile mill in the country, and serves as a reminder of the city's industrial history.

Meredith is a quintessential New England town located at the northwest corner of Lake Winnipesaukee. It boasts many fine stores, hotels, and the popular Summer Theatre in Meredith Village.

From the summit of Mount Morgan, hikers following the Morgan-Percival Loop may gaze southward over the lake and hill country, and northward to New Hampshire's higher peaks.

Dogsled races on Chocorua Lake have a long history and provide a popular spectator sport during the long winter months.

Fishermen try their luck until sunset on the beaches of Lake Winnisquam, whose waters abound with rainbow and lake trout, salmon, bass, pickerel, and white perch.

The Inn on Golden Pond, a cheerful bed and breakfast that occupies a large 1870s-era house, sits on 50 wooded acres near Squam Lake, otherwise known as Golden Pond. The inn was the setting for the film "On Golden Pond."

The haunting call of the loon echoes across the Lakes Region during the summer months, although it disappears when the birds move to the seacoast for the winter.

Measuring six miles long and more than two miles wide, Newfound Lake is the third-largest lake in New Hampshire.

In addition to growing flowers and produce, Longhaul Farm in Holderness hosts a "taste of the farm" meal with live music in early July.

Spectacular views from the summit of Mount Major in Alton make this challenging hike well worth the effort. On a clear day Mount Washington can be seen approximately 50 miles to the north.

Waterskiers, boaters, and fishermen alike enjoy Squam Lake's placid summer waters and clear views of West Rattlesnake Mountain.

Lilacs are the official state flower of New Hampshire. Many shrubs come into bloom during late May such as these which adorn a quaint New England homestead between Hebron and Plymouth.

Winter wonderland comes to this classic New England barn found in Hebron.

White Mountains

Stretching northeastward from Mount Moosilauke, the White Mountains march in a ragged, diagonal line across New Hampshire. As their anchor, Mount Washington—the highest point in New England—has attracted tourists to the Granite State for more than 150 years. Its popular hiking trails, auto road, and cog railway entertain visitors during the warm months. In winter, outdoor enthusiasts flock to the White Mountains' ski resorts and backcountry destinations like Tuckerman Ravine to enjoy this vast wilderness area.

Built in 1858 and renovated in 1970, the Kancamagus Highway's Albany Covered Bridge spans the Swift River near the Boulder Loop Nature Trail and the White Mountain National Forest Covered Bridge Campground.

Named for a great Seminole chief, Mount Osceola is a dominant feature of Waterville Valley. When viewed from the Kancamagus Highway, the slide scars on its northern flank are an impressive sight.

With Mount Adams and Mount Madison in the background, the Mount Washington Auto Road climbs beside the alpine flowers of early June—white diapensia and purple Lapland rosebay.

Franconia Notch's Lonesome Lake provides a cool resting place for both day hikers and for overnight guests in the nearby Appalachian Mountain Club hut.

Anchoring the southwest corner of the White Mountains, Mount Moosilauke is a hikers' favorite with its magnificent traverse from the South Peak to the main summit, as well as its numerous other trails, all maintained by Dartmouth College.

This lupine field on Sugar Hill teems with the purple, pink and white blossoms that fill New Hampshire's meadows and highway medians every June.

Mount Washington's Tuckerman Ravine is reflected in Hermit Lake.

Since its opening in 1902, the Mount Washington Hotel in Bretton Woods has drawn vacationers to its elegant rooms, extensive network of trails, and golf course that rolls beneath the Presidential Range.

The sweeping vista of the Northern Presidential Range presides over the snow-covered fields of Jefferson Meadows, a traditional summer vacation retreat.

The Appalachian Mountain Club's Highland Center, an outdoor education and recreation facility in Crawford Notch welcomes visitors to the White Mountains throughout the year.

Nine miles by trail from the nearest road and deep in the Pemigewasset Wilderness, the 4,265-foot summit of Bondcliff reveals no sign of human civilization.

Covering 90 acres of the Pondicherry National Wildlife Refuge, Cherry Pond is known for its abundance of birds, unusual bog vegetation, and sweeping views of the Presidential Range.

From the Rim Trail on the summit of Cannon Mountain, Mount Lafayette and Mount Lincoln define Franconia Ridge, one of the classic hikes of the eastern United States.

Scientists at the Mount Washington Observatory study all aspects of meteorology, including those that create the summit's sculpted snow formations.

Visible from the four-mile mark of the Mount Washington Auto Road, the Great Gulf Wilderness is one of many glacial cirques in the White Mountains.

From late March into June, Tuckerman Ravine attracts thousands of skiers, sledders, and spectators to its steep headwall and snow-filled bowl.

In winter, ice formations cover the 90-foot granite cliffs of the Flume—a chasm carved by Flume Brook, drawing many climbers to Franconia Notch.

Kayakers paddle a calm stretch of the Pemigewasset River river between the towns of Lincoln and Thorton.

Located on the grounds of the Mount Washington Hotel, the Bretton Woods Nordic Center boasts 100 kilometers of ski trails, nearly all tracked and groomed, making the resort one of the finest in New England.

Built in 1865, the 200-room Mountain View Grand Hotel in Whitefield welcomed summer guests to the region for more than a century before closing its doors. The hotel reopened in 2002 after extensive renovations, once again thrilling visitors with its spectacular views of the Presidential Range.

To reach the 2,605-foot summit of Welch Mountain, which overlooks Waterville Valley, hikers navigate the granite slabs and exposed bedrock of the Welch-Dickey Loop Trail.

Forming the southern wall of Tuckerman Ravine, the steep flanks of Boott Spur tempt spring skiers with routes like Hillman's Highway.

Since its opening in 1869, the Mount Washington Cog Railway has carried countless passengers up the mountain's steep slope using a unique cogwheel system that provides both traction and braking.

The Flume Covered Bridge was originally built in 1886 and spans the Pemigewasset River in the Flume area of Franconia Notch State Park. Covered bridges were often called "kissing bridges" because of the darkness and privacy they provided.

With its clear view of Mount Carrigain and the eastern Pemigewasset Wilderness, many hikers consider Zeacliff Outlook the finest promontory in the White Mountains.

Waterfalls

While neither terribly high nor powerful, New Hampshire's waterfalls are famous for their great number and variety. In the White Mountains in particular, rainfall and snowmelt feed streams that plunge over cliffs, glisten on sheer rock faces, and cut narrow ravines into the mountainsides. On gentler slopes, the waterfalls wind around mossy boulders, forming calm pools and deep swimming holes. With their striking natural beauty and cool, clear water, New Hampshire's cascades attract both photographers and weary hikers.

This cascade lies about one mile up the Smarts Brook Trail in Waterville Valley, just an easy walk from Route 49.

After hiking a short distance from the Kancamagus Highway, visitors can use a series of walkways to view Sabbaday Falls from several dramatic angles.

The cold waters of the Ammonoosuc River create whirlpool currents beneath the Upper Ammonoosuc Falls, drawing summer visitors to this scenic swimming hole in Bretton Woods.

Arethusa Falls, New Hampshire's highest waterfall, is framed with ice formations as winter sets in on Crawford Notch.

Crystal Cascade falls 80 feet in two drops, tucked between cliffs shaded by spruce, fir, birch, and mountain ash on the Tuckerman Ravine Trail in Pinkham Notch.

Bridal Veil Falls is a graceful waterfall located off the Coppermine Trail in Easton, New Hampshire. The 80-foot falls are a 2.5-mile hike in from the trailhead.

Located off Magalloway Road in Pittsburg, Garfield Falls forms a 40-foot drop in the East Branch of the Dead Diamond River. As a major obstacle to the great nineteenth-century log drives down the Androscoggin River, the waterfall's unique formation of rock walls once caused many log jams.

Located near the eastern entrance to Crawford Notch State Park, Arethusa Falls is New Hampshire's highest waterfall at 200 feet. It is a one-and-a-half-mile hike in from Route 302.

Gleason Falls Road in Hillsborough runs beside Beard Brook, which tips over Gleason Falls in a slender cascade of sparkling white water.

North Country

New Hampshire's narrow, northernmost region, the 1,855 square miles of Coös County, is larger than Rhode Island. Visitors to this sparsely populated area may spot moose grazing or fall asleep to the haunting call of loons. The region's vast forests and the headwaters of the Connecticut and the Androscoggin Rivers attract fishermen, paddlers, hunters, and snowmobilers. Numerous campgrounds as well as two grand nineteenth-century resort hotels welcome vacationers to this pristine corner of New Hampshire.

Small dairy farms dot the landscape between Colebrook and Pittsburg—one of the first areas in New Hampshire to change color in the fall.

Unknown Pond rests beneath the peak of The Horn on a high plateau in the Kilkenny region of northern New Hampshire.

A popular destination for fishermen, hunters, and snowmobilers, the shores of First Connecticut Lake in Pittsburg are sprinkled with lodges and cabins along Route 3.

Lake Gloriette reflects the grand hotel at The Balsams Resort and the superb fall foliage of Dixville Notch.

Pond Brook collects the waters of many remote ponds and small streams, draining more than 120 acres of highland shelf feeding these falls in Nash Stream valley.

Route 26 winds through Dixville Notch 700 feet below the narrow precipice of Table Rock.

During World War II, German prisoners of war worked in a woods camp not far from Stark's picturesque union church and 1850s covered bridge.

According to legend, Lost Nation Road received its name from a traveling preacher who likened the local folks to the lost tribes of Israel when he managed to persuade only one person between Lancaster and Groveton to attend church.

A full-grown bull moose can be seven feet at the shoulder and weigh 1000 to 1200 pounds.

Concord and South

While the urban communities of the Merrimack Valley cannot boast the vast wilderness acreage of the White Mountains, southern New Hampshire offers its own unique treasures and rich history. Concord's elegant legislative building and the old mills of Manchester form a picture of the cities' beginnings. Both Manchester and the state capital boast thriving downtown districts with many fine restaurants, theaters, and art galleries. Between these bustling cities, many small, picturesque towns lie hidden just a short detour off the highway.

Gould Hill Orchards, a 200-year-old family farm in Contoocook, offers a winding nature trail as well as an orchard store filled with cider, baked goods, peaches, maple syrup, and 87 varieties of apples.

Built in 1845, Manchester's Gothic-style city hall contrasts sharply with the modern building behind.

The tiny village of Washington includes an 1840s Gothic-style church, a two-story 1830s schoolhouse, and a meetinghouse completed in 1789, all clustered on the north side of the common.

The passing of seasons in a Nashua cemetery reminds one of the city's ancestors.

Spanning Gleason Falls in Hillsborough, this freestanding granite bridge displays the precision and artistry of the area's nineteenth-century Irish and Scottish stonemasons.

The poet Robert Frost lived in this 1880s clapboard house in Derry between 1900 and 1909, when he did much of his writing. Today, an interpretive nature trail runs through the surrounding woods and fields, even passing by Frost's "mending wall."

The New Hampshire State House in Concord is the oldest state capitol whose legislature still meets in its original chambers, which date from 1819.

Monadnock Region

Towering 2,000 feet above the hills of southwestern New Hampshire, Mount Monadnock is visible for up to 50 miles in every direction. Crisscrossed with rushing streams, the region's 40 towns once flourished with small mills. Today, these nineteenth-century relics blend in with the narrow roads, villages of white clapboard houses, and tall, steepled churches. Not only did Thoreau and Emerson feature Mount Monadnock in several of their 1850s works, but the town of Peterborough inspired Thornton Wilder to write *Our Town*.

Perkins Pond in Jaffrey lies within sight of Mount Monadnock—an Algonquin word for "mountain that stands alone."

With its little cluster of brick, granite, and white-trimmed buildings perched beside a millpond, the community of Harrisville echoes New England's earliest villages.

Marlow is a charming New England village which comes alive with color during the fall foliage season.

After years of planting orchards, pasturing sheep, building stonewalls, and logging hardwood and spruce from Monadnock's lower flanks, early settlers began to burn its summit slopes in hopes of killing off the wolves. Today, alpine flora endure on the mountain's bald peak.

The centerpiece of Jaffrey is its tall, white meetinghouse built in 1773—now the site of a summer lecture series called the Amos Fortune Forum.

Willa Cather spent many summers at the Shattuck Inn in Jaffrey Center, writing two of her best novels—My Antonia and Death Comes to the Archbishop.

Keene, the shire town of Cheshire County, boasts the widest Main Street in New England.

The Cresson Covered Bridge is one of four covered bridges found in the Monadnock town of Swanzey.

Mount Monadnock dominates the rolling landscape of southwestern New Hampshire; it is as much a part of the surrounding towns as their meetinghouse steeples.

The Upper Valley

The Connecticut River Valley flourishes thanks to its fertile bottomland and the cultural center of Dartmouth College. Recently designated one of America's scenic byways, the region abounds with picturesque villages, working landscapes, and tourist attractions. One of America's longest covered bridges, spans the river between Cornish, New Hampshire and Windsor, Vermont. During its 410-mile journey from its source on the Québec border to Long Island Sound, the Connecticut River nourishes the land and culture of a growing, dynamic region.

Spanning the Connecticut River with its 1866 lattice truss design, the Windsor-Cornish Bridge is the longest wooden bridge in the United States and the longest two-span bridge in the world.

Handsome academic buildings such as Baker Memorial Library—a 1920s version of Philadelphia's Independence Hall—frame three sides of the Dartmouth College green, while the fourth side includes a large inn, an arts center, and an outstanding art museum.

Dartmouth Row, a line of four striking colonial-era buildings on the eastern edge of the green, comprised Dartmouth College in its entirety from the school's charter in 1769 until 1845.

Built in 1906, this round barn in Piermont dates from the height of the design's popularity. During the late nineteenth and early twentieth centuries, agricultural schools promoted both circular and octagonal barns as efficient, labor-saving structures with high volume-to-surface area ratios.

For three generations, the Minot family has operated this dairy farm in Bath and sugared the surrounding hills.

The historic community of Haverhill Corner centers around a large village green ringed with Federal and Greek Revival homes and public buildings.

This beautiful 1832 covered bridge and the neighboring 1804 Old Brick Store—"America's oldest general store"—draw visitors to the village of Bath.

Sunset on Lake Winnisquam.